Lessons Learned Learning Medicine

J. B. DURAND

MD, FACC, FACP, FCCP, FAHA, FHFSA, FESC, FHRS, FHFA, FRCP

Published by:

OWL® PUBLISHERS

www.owlpublishers.com

360 S Market St, San Jose, CA 95113,
United States.

Printed in the United States of America

Dedication

The best day of my life was the day my children were born, when I held each of them in my arms and felt the world stop.

The second-best day of my life was the day I became an American citizen, a moment that marked belonging, responsibility, and possibility.

Most of us move through life having experiences first and understanding the lessons later. These lessons are written for my children, so they may carry the wisdom before the experience.

Acknowledgments

I dedicate this book to the individuals who shaped my life and education.

Dr. Kenneth Marsi, thank you for your patience in teaching me college organic chemistry. You believed in me, and ultimately, I believed in myself.

Dr. Roger Acey, thank you for teaching me the foundations of biochemistry and showing me that biochemistry ultimately accounts for all of life's processes.

Dr. Rolf Gunner, your belief in basic research and your decision to allow me to take one year off from my residency became the tipping point of my career.

Dr. Maria Rosa Costanzo, the first female transplant cardiologist in Chicago at Loyola University—thank you for teaching me never to give up on patients and to cultivate an impenetrable will to save a life through knowledge and compassion.

Dr. Al Samarel taught me molecular biology, animal research, protein chemistry, and research methods.

Dr. Robert Roberts introduced me to the world of inherited molecular genetics of heart disease and supported my education.

Dr. Joseph Swafford and Dr. Harry Gibbs taught me the language of administration.

My sisters, Nadya Curtis and Rachelle Espinosa, were always present, offering wisdom and light when all I could see was darkness.

My parents, Jean Michael Durand and Celide Durand, instilled in me the four pillars of my life: faith, education, work ethic, and family values. I understood the sacrifices immigrant parents make for their children. To lessen their burden and allow them to reach retirement, I put myself through college. I never feared my parents physically, but throughout my life I feared disappointing them.

Appreciation to all of my patients who taught me the meaning of resilience and how to live each day, knowing tomorrow may never come.

Foreword

My life experiences have never been about the destination; they have always been about the journey and the person I would become along the way.

From my children, I learned the importance of selflessness over selfishness. Everything I am and have accomplished was for them, not for myself, as part of a greater calling.

To the world, I am their father. To me, my children are my world.

Preface

"We are all born in the darkest of ignorance, and the light of knowledge awakened my life."

The best day of my life was when my children were born.

And the day I swore in as an American citizen

The four pillars of my life:

Family | **Work Ethics** | **Education** | **Faith**

Day 1

"**Life** is challenging but also **beautiful**; embrace the difficulties, appreciate its **beauty**."

Day 2

"The **world** can be **gray**, not **black** and **white**."

Day 3

"There is no **right** way to do something **wrong**."

Day 4

"**Stress** comes from doing something you do not **want** to be doing."

Day 5

"We often confuse others' **honesty** with **bitterness**."

Day 6

"We do not worry enough about our **character** and too much about our **reputation**. Our **character** is who we really are, our core values, our integrity, and our own personal mission statement. Our **reputation** is based on what others think of us."

Day 7

"If you make a **decision** for the right **reasons**... no matter how much it hurts, you have made the right **decision**."

Day 8

"My parents were right, saying **thank you, please, excuse me**, as well as beginning and ending a sentence with **yes, sir**, and **no, ma'am**, will get you **extraordinarily** far in this **world**."

Day 9

"It's better to be **alone** and **happy** than to be **married**, **lonely**, and **miserable**."

Day 10

"**Arrogance** and **self-awareness** rarely go together."

Day 11

"Our **personalities** are the sum of our life **experiences** and the people we surround ourselves with."

Day 12

"Most of us are more afraid of **living** than **dying**."

Day 13

"Everyone should experience a **death** in a public place (I know this is dark) to witness life leaving this earth is **transformational**, and forces one to assess the importance of life."

Day 14

"Just because I don't **understand** you that does not make you an **artist**."

Day 15

"**Stress** is not the same for everyone; some individuals apparently have a large capacity to **tolerate** and **manage stress**."

Day 16

"We exist throughout our **lives** as two individuals: the **person** we are, and the person we can become. We should make it our **mission that those two people encounter** on our **journey**."

Day 17

"Sometimes you have to make the **wrong** choices in life to get you to the **right** places."

Day 18

"Mark Twain once said that two of the most important days in your life are the day that you were **born** and the day you find out **why**."

Day 19

"If you predict **bad** things consistently, eventually you will be **right**."

Day 20

"There is no substitute for the **truth**, no matter how **ugly** it may be."

Day 21

"The one thing that will keep a team from reaching its full **potential** is **'Meetings'**."

Day 22

"Do not **confuse** your practice with your **life**."

Day 23

"No one **cares** about you as much as you **think** they do."

Day 24

"Never, ever, say anything to a **woman** that suggests that you think she may be pregnant unless you happen to be in the operating room assisting with her **vaginal** or **C-section delivery**."

Day 25

"A person who is **pleasant** to you, but an ass to a **waiter** or **waitress**, is not a nice person. (You should make this observation and **remember** it time and again."

Day 26

"To **rely** on others is to be **disappointed**."

Day 27

"We all **see** life through the filter of our previous **experiences**."

Day 28

"**Never** is no longer in my vocabulary, except this: I will never be able to **express** the depth of my **love** for my children."

Day 29

"The ancient saying, 'Sticks and stones may hurt my bones, but words will never hurt me.' My life **experiences** have taught me that 'The pain of a stick will always go away and heal, but words are **divisive**, **painful**, and are **eternal**.'"

Day 30

"What we say and what we do can be very different from what we believe. **True**, **authentic growth** comes from **saying**, **believing**, and doing the same."

Day 31

"Corporate culture paradox: If you see something, say something, yet if you define a **problem**, you become the **problem**."

Day 32

"**Leadership** can be more about becoming something you aren't than **becoming** something you are."

Day 33

"Sometimes one's heart **hurts** too much to be **angry**."

Day 34

"The **corporate circle** has a unique underbelly: 'live inside the circle and know everything, and to survive you feel nothing, or live outside the circle and know nothing, and to **survive** you feel **everything**.'"

Day 35

"In **God** we **trust**; everything else, we need data."

Day 36

"Just because **you** can do it doesn't mean **you** should do it."

Day 37

"I'd rather live one day as a **lion** than 1000 days as a **lamb**."

Day 38

"Is it just **me**, or does **Ben Carson** speak like he is one scalpel short of an operation?"

Day 39

"The voice of **ten angry** people is far more influential than the voice of the **1000 silent majority**."

Day 40

"Someone once said, '**Imagine** a world in which we are all **enlightened** by objective truths rather than offended by them.'"

Day 41

"There will be **times** in our career where the doors of **opportunity** remain forever **closed**, and you will need to **'kick** the door down.'"

Day 42

"Can **honestly** state that I am overweight and need to lose ten pounds, but I identify as skinny."

Day 43

"I am at a point in my **life** that I find myself continuously asking, 'Which **battles** of my associates do I want to fight today? Which of their **demons** do I want to avoid **engaging**?"

Day 44

"There are a lot of very **talented people** out there who will never reach their level of success because their inner **demons** or **external demons** constantly prey on their success."

Day 45

"You are in trouble if you give me the **'silent treatment,'** and I enjoy it."

Day 46

"Outside of the hospital, I am not the guy who feels a need to validate my **adulthood** by fixing everything. I am ok with that. Now, get **help**, own, and fix your own **dysfunctions**."

Day 47

"My **life's** work outside of the hospital is not to **validate** you, I will listen to you, **support** you, and **love** you, deal with your own shit, or let that shit go!!"

Day 48

"We continuously run from our inner **demons**, never understanding that our inner **demons** are ever present, lurk in the shadows, and find unfortunate, untimely, and **painful** ways to confront us."

Day 49

"Living your **life** to fit into a **tribe** is overrated."

Day 50

"Most of the unfinished **business** in your **life** can always be found in a cemetery."

Day 51

"I get it, **life** is not **binary**."

Day 52

"**Failure** can be **success**."

Day 53

"I have become **comfortable** with the **daily** grind and not seeing much **progress**."

Day 54

"We **live** in a culture that screams out **failures** and **whispers accomplishments**. Is that **humility** or **insecurity**?"

Day 55

"From **hardship** comes **enlightenment**."

Day 56

"If you don't **love** yourself, you cannot **love** me."

Day 57

"**Fear** and **faith** cannot exist together."

Day 58

"If you are **depressed**, you live in the past; if you are **anxious**, you live in the future."

Day 59

"I have lost many times in **life**, but I have learned to **appreciate** the times I have won."

Day 60

"Don't worry about **karma**; it is always waiting for you **outside** your **door**."

Day 61

"As we **age**, we learn that **life's** journey is one we get to write; it's about the choices we make and the **responsibility** we take for them."

Day 62

"It takes far more **courage** to confront your inner **demons** than to run from them."

Day 63

"**Truth** does not become more **true** by virtue of the fact that the entire world agrees with it, nor less so even if the whole world **disagrees** with it."

Day 64

"Is it just **me**, or does **Joe Biden a**ppear to be a few candles short of a **Menorah**?"

Day 65

"**Society** spends far too much time focusing on **strengths** and **refuses** to look at weaknesses. I have been acknowledging my strengths, but spend more time and effort working on my **weaknesses**. I can always do **better** and be a **better** person."

Day 66

"I am the **person** I was meant to be, and I am all **right** with this."

Day 67

"Sometimes in my **life**, I had to get burned more than once to learn not to **touch** a hot stove."

Day 68

"Get to know me **real** well because you will not meet a man like me **twice** in your **life**."

Day 69

"The purpose of **life** is to **live**, to experience **love**, **pain**, **heartache**, to name a few; to deny these experiences is only to **exist**."

Day 70

"Everyone has a **right** to **success**, but not everyone is entitled to **success**."

Day 71

"Sometimes in your work **life**, you will more likely get a **stick** than a carrot."

Day 72

"My **views** about the world around me are continuously **changing**, as my **experiences** in **life** change, my **values** remain intact."

Day 73

"I have had to **work** very hard throughout my **life** to approach **life** with no **fear** and no **ego**, I have had to do this because in my **career**, those with **egos** and **fear** have always tried to **hijack** my **life**."

Day 74

"You cannot have a **healthy**, **functional relationship** in your future if you are still held **hostage** to your **past emotional** pains."

Day 75

"Healing from previous **emotional** pains is a lifelong process; sometimes it requires leaving the **environment** that hurt you in the first place."

Day 76

"Physical injuries all **heal** in time and leave a well-healed **scar**; emotional pains can never heal, unless courageously **confronted** and **conquered**."

Day 77

"Your most crucial superhero **power** is to decide how you choose to cherish your **emotional** gardens, both rain and **sunshine** make **flowers** grow."

Day 78

"Listen to people, really listen to your **inner voice**, then watch their **behavior**; your **inner voice** will always tell you something is just not right."

Day 79

"In this season of my **life**, I have met many people who have accumulated a lifetime of minor **pains**; a ton of leaves is still a ton."

Day 80

"It takes tremendous inner **strength** and **courage** to face our emotional **fears**."

Day 81

"**Humor** is derived in the face of **pain**."

Day 82

"I know I have **grown** when I was asked the other day, 'What is the most valuable to **you**?' I answered, **'Self-knowledge**.'"

Day 83

"I lost my **desire** to care what people **think** of me early in my **adult** life. When I was in college, my capacity to believe that it is really none of my business what **people think** about me, and to stay laser focused on being the **best version** of **myself**, consumed my psyche."

Day 84

"When I am doing a heart procedure, I can make it appear **effortless**, **simple**, and very **natural** in my hands, until the fellow attempts it and it seems **awkward**, like a teenage girl trying to walk in stilettos. What few appreciate are the millions of times I rehearsed every motion, every step in my mind while shaving, in the shower, or when I let my mind **daydream**, and the thousands of heart procedures I have performed over my **career**. It reminds me of the ignorance of our society that fails to understand the many gifted **musicians**, **songstresses**, **artists** who perfected their craft from thousands of hours and many years of work."

Day 85

"I **learned** and **validated** early in life that problems left unresolved become **crises** later in **life**."

Day 86

"Crises in our **lives** are an emotional **stress** test; they expose the small, vulnerable spaces in our foundation and our resilience. These help to fill in our **weaknesses** in our **emotional** foundation and make us better prepared for **future** challenges."

Day 87

"What is it about **humanity** that we believe in the ideology of **overnight success**? Successful people, when fully transparent, will tell you it's not overnight, it's 'over **your whole life**'!!!"

Day 88

"When I thought I was at the end of an **experience**, I was already at the **beginning** of another."

Day 89

"Your **life** is a canvas; you are in complete **control** of what you produce."

Day 90

"I saw this sign at work: 'The **beatings** will continue until **morale** improves.'"

- Anonymous

Day 91

"Unfortunately, in **life**, doing **really great** work frequently goes **unnoticed**."

Day 92

"I still **struggle** with this. I hardly ever celebrate what I have **accomplished**; I am always looking forward to what **needs** to be completed."

Day 93

"Important **life** lesson: 'I don't know, but **I will** find out.'"

Day 94

"For every mistake you have made in **life**, forgive **yourself**."

Day 95

"**Self-confidence** does not come from **reading** or **thinking** you are unique. Your confidence comes from your **body of work** with **blood**, **sweat**, and **tears** that are the foundation of who you are."

Day 96

Maya Angelou said "Learn to **love** yourself and appreciate time alone to reflect on **who you are**, what you **believe**, what you will stand for, and what you will not stand for."

Day 97

"Apparently, as it relates to **leadership**, I am an easy person to read but a tough **person** to get to know (I don't like to talk about being unapologetically **myself**.")

Day 98

"When a **person** shows you who they are, you have to **believe** them."

- Maya Angelou

Day 99

"You know what's great about this time of my **life**? Being **unapologetic myself**."

Day 100

"A day without overcoming **obstacles** is a day filled with **regret**."

Day 101

"Every day of my **life**, I have seen patients be **courageous** in the face of their greatest **fears**."

Day 102

"As **you** get **older**, stay away from people your age if you don't want to get **older**. (There are exceptions, you know who **you** are."

Day 103

"It is so much easier to **judge** people than to **understand** them."

Day 104

"Do we appreciate **memories** after they pass? Can't we learn to **enjoy** the present right now?"

Day 105

"I have accepted my many **imperfections**; one is that, until my last breath, I never **engage** when I hear the phrase, 'it's just not **fair'**. My inner voice is saying, 'Who in your life waterboarded you into believing that life is **fair**?' If life were **fair** for me, every time I had a good outcome with my **patients**, an administrator would hand me a soft-serve ice cream cone."

Day 106

"**Life** experiences can be so intense. Yes, my sense of humor can be a bit off. I don't comment to be mean; I comment because I find **humor** in the **ridiculous**."

Day 107

"Let's pretend you like your **local** or **national** politician."

Day 108

"Surrounding yourself with people who **struggle**, have **visions**, and **aim** to be better in life promotes **success**. Surrounding yourself with people who don't ask the best of you means you **live** in a **cage**."

Day 109

"**Birkenstocks** are an unusual form of **birth** control (think about this for a while."

Day 110

"I have had times in my **life** when I had no **luck**, such that if I sold candles, the sun would never set."

Day 111

"At this time of my **life**, I am tired of **complainers**. I know and understand their brand. I choose to focus and express gratitude. This has helped me to see the **good** qualities of those in my inner circle. There is **freedom** in accepting how blessed one can be, especially when **life** gets **difficult**."

Day 112

"We are in an **age** of immediate gratification. The cost of my **success** was paid several decades before I became a tenured **professor**."

Day 113

"I recently heard this quote:

'The day you plant the seed is not the day you eat the fruit.'"

- Anonymous

Day 114

"There are a lot of very talented people in **life** who will never reach their level of **success** because of their inner **demons** or **external demons** that constantly prey on their success."

Day 115

"The **world** would be a better place if we could all agree to take **ownership** of our own shit."

Day 116

"I can't fix your **shit** because I have enough of my own **shit** to fix."

Day 117

"Sometimes **life** is going to **kick** you in the ass."

Day 118

"Brave leaders are never silent about **complex**, **controversial issues** or **conversations**."

Day 119

"**Faith** and **hope**, not past **pains**, **guide** my future."

Day 120

"I have a better understanding of who I am by learning and understanding my past **mistakes**, so that I can **live** my **future** with more **joy**."

Day 121

"This is an excellent season of my **life** when I can look at my **physical** and **emotional** scars and own who I am."

Day 122

"I can now compartmentalize my **life**: The first years of my **life** were the age of **innocence**. The following years of my life were the age of **enlightenment**. The next years of my life were the age of **darkness**. I am in the present phase. How will I choose to acknowledge those years?"

Day 123

"Do not be upset with how far you went in your **career** without consideration of the **time** and **work** you committed to your **success**."

Day 124

"**Memories** of our **loved** ones are eternal. My mother died several years ago; to this day, I still pick up the phone to talk to her when she was not ill. My favorite used to be when she was talking and I said something to her with my dark sense of humor, she was well into her following paragraph when she realized what an inappropriate thing I just said, and she would laugh a side-splitting laugh while I heard her thoughts of 'my son is just not right.'"

Day 125

"My most recent epiphany: Relationships with **friends**, **coworkers**, **bosses**, **family**, and **spouses** are not created to drain you **emotionally**, although I take into account the day-to-day **struggles** of all of the above, **authentic** functional relationships are more about deriving mutual **strength** and **support**."

Day 126

"**Corporate culture** is fascinating. They express mission statements and policies for **sexual harassment**, **inclusion**, **diversity**, and **retaliation**. These principles take the form of repeated narratives that, when repeated enough times, can institutionalize and radicalize an employee into believing they are true. Yet the very leadership that wrote them frequently violated them."

Day 127

"**Quitting** a job is OK. **Moving** on is OK. **Struggling** is OK. **Leaving** a **Toxic relationship** or **job** is OK. Staying in any situation, work or personal, where you are not valued or appreciated?-No Bueno!!!!!!!!!!!!!"

Day 128

"Someone's **behavior** towards me is irrelevant to me; I now understand that my presence can provoke their **own internal struggles** that have nothing to do with me."

Day 129

"We say wonderful things about **friends**, **family**, and **loved ones** at funerals. Why is the human condition so programmed not to say these comments at our birthdays? There is so much we want to speak to them, but we are reluctant."

Day 130

"With my college education, I **learned** how to learn and realized I knew little. Through **life** experiences, I learned how to apply **knowledge** and gained **wisdom**."

Day 131

"**Physical** and **emotional** traumas can silence an individual or drive them to great heights; only you have the power to decide."

Day 132

"When you permit someone to make you **bitter**, **sad**, or **angry**, 'they own you.'"

Day 133

"Sometimes, I am **kidding/not kidding**. You need to see the look on my face when I say this to you."

Day 134

"I don't remember what age or how many times I remind **myself** that if you want a behavior to continue, reward it."

Day 135

"**Diversity** in the corporate world is a paradox. The narrative is based on the ideology that **race**, **gender**, and **sexual orientation** are welcome in the corporate world. My views about this have never been in concordance with corporate values. Diversity to me is not about any **traditional** definition; it's about the diversity of **thought**. The underbelly of the diversity of thought is counterintuitive to the corporate culture of having the same opinions, beliefs, and mannerisms to be accepted in the circle."

Day 136

"M & M (morbidity and mortality, a tradition in medicine during the informative years of my medical training, no longer exists in today's world. The event was always held very early in the morning and presented by junior residents to junior and senior faculty. The meetings involved a synopsis of patients' cases with complications, including deaths. The sessions were intense and required your ability to withstand extreme criticism and ridicule. Only those with the most complicated **emotional** armor can withstand the level of disapproval by the **public**, pointing out one's faults. **'Wimps need not apply**.'"

Day 137

"A **title** or a corner office in a C-suite does not guarantee you **respect** or influence from those who report to you."

Day 138

"I have had far too many medical **decisions** that I have had to make alone. Apparently, I can challenge the central dogma with calculated risk. Over twenty years ago, there was one example of a woman destined to **die** shortly. Her family made plans to transfer her to hospice. A well-trained friend of mine was recruited to work with me. She asked me why I was starting this woman on medications when she was headed to hospice to die. No one on any team or the nurses on the floor supported my decision. When requested to present my decision to the team meeting, I was delighted to present my argument. I knew there was no argument about medical care, so I decided to present a narrative of moral hazard. Ethics: 'It is our fiduciary responsibility to not only provide healthcare but also reduce pain and suffering as we transition our patients to the afterlife.' I kept my stone face and did not raise my voice because I understood that if I yelled, most people would seek shelter. So my tone was that of my inner Steve Sherman, when he played for the Seattle Seahawks. 'Don't you ever disrespect me,' I told them. I discussed this with our patient; the goal was not to prolong her life; the treatment was intended to allow her to breathe more comfortably so that she would not gasp for air, but to die a comfortable death with dignity. Forty-eight hours later, she was **smiling** and **breathing** comfortably for her transfer to hospice."

Day 139

"We all **see** the world differently. We can also be utterly **blind** to the world around us."

Day 140

"I have been **astonished** by how many of my women colleagues have described a stare from male counterparts that treats them like puzzles they don't want to put **together**."

Day 141

"You know you are in a toxic **relationship** if you have ever considered enhanced interrogation techniques to get your **significant** other to speak the **truth**."

Day 142

"**Knowledge** is really about building a foundational base camp so that by the time you reach the summit of your **life**, forks on the ascent or **potholes** are met with confidence."

Day 143

"I still do not understand what I have **learned** from this observation: A very handsome man walks into a room. Men: 'I need to get to the gym, work on my hair, and my suits.' A tall, beautiful woman walks into a room. Women: 'I need to grab my machete out of my Michael Kors handbag, chop off her appendages, and hide the body.' **I cannot wrap my mind around this. Why."**

Day 144

"Blind **allegiance** and **obedience** to a relationship, **corporation**, or **government**? What happens when our own values and ethos conflict with institutions? I have never struggled to just say No!!! How do we manage? **Stay**, **reject**, or **leave**?"

Day 145

"There is a difference between what you **think**, what you **feel**, and the **truth**. Many times in life, these do not line up."

Day 146

"I am on the back nine of **my career**, looking at what I discovered and changed in the practice of medicine, the odds of my accomplishments are one in a billion."

Day 147

"It takes a lifetime of experience to develop insight and **self-awareness**, yet some people go to their grave never knowing who they are or their values."

Day 148

"There have been days in my **life** when I have walked through the door of my home, and **joyful** that I am still **alive**, it's a **triumph**."

Day 149

"Women in **corporate leadership** are visible, yet **invisible** (take some time to think about this."

Day 150

"**Failure** in the early years of your life is the foundation for future **success**."

Day 151

"Every man at some point in his **life** has a sentinel event that he decides: Am I a sheep? A **predator** or a **protector**? Once he figures this out, he will be prepared to choose his **destiny**."

Day 152

"If you have something bad to say about me, **tell** it to my face, and I will **respect** your courage. Say something bad about me behind my back, and you will never **forgive** me for what I tell you to your face and behind your back."

Day 153

"Remember the old saying, Life is not **fair**? Since early adulthood, I learned that 'life is **fair** because it's **unfair** to everyone.'"

Day 154

"There will be **experiences** during your **life** when you feel you have been torn apart into a billion pieces, put back together. Suddenly, **you** realize you have **superpowers** and can **overcome** anything."

Day 155

"You will never be **good** enough for the **wrong** person."

- Anonymous

Day 156

"**Pain** and **suffering** are a part of human existence. However, it is not the purpose of our **lives**."

Day 157

"When we are young, we believe that **life** exists as **rainbows** and **unicorns** until we learn it's messy, has many **peaks** and **valleys**, and a series of revelations."

Day 158

"We experience events in our **lives** and conclude with a period. We really should place a comma to reflect the continuum of our **lives**."

Day 159

"One of the greatest **fears** for either spouse in a relationship is having the courage to **ask** for what they need."

Day 160

"You cannot reach the pinnacle of any **success** without knowing the **humility** of being in the valleys of your **journey**."

Day 161

"Relationships can be **easy** or **difficult**; we decide individually based on our **ego**, **pride**, and **unacknowledged** past deficiencies that haunt those who care about **us**."

Day 162

"Many people are **smart** enough to make it through medical school and can become physicians. What separates the great and gifted ones is the ability to withstand the **stress** and **pressure** of making **life-or-death** decisions in seconds to minutes of assessing a **life-or-death** situation."

Day 163

"One of the most **rewarding** days of my life was when my children were born, and I looked into their eyes and the **world** disappeared."

Day 164

"**Fear**? 'There is nothing in the **nighttime** that was not there in the **daytime**.'"

Day 165

"In some families, **trouble** comes by the **pound**."

Day 166

"My life could be **worse**; I could have **married** Amber Heard."

Day 167

"I heard this **quote** today, and I do not remember the author, so I apply it outside of medicine. When I work from my **heart**, **everything** works; when I work from my **head**, **nothing** works."

Day 168

"Sometimes people confuse my **kindness** with **weakness** or **meekness**. In Greek, meek means **'strength under control**.'"

Day 169

"**Growth** comes from **struggles** in life's journey."

Day 170

"You never know your **true**, **authentic** self in life's journey until you have been pushed to the outer boundaries of your **physical**, **mental**, and **emotional** capabilities."

Day 171

"There is a version of **you** created by others that they only want to see. The **disappointment** of others is when they discover **they** were wrong."

Day 172

"Being in a relationship with a **narcissist**, a **passive-aggressive**, or someone with **low emotional intelligence** is similar to being pulled into a **tornado** and **quicksand**. Their inner demons will draw you into their **vortex** and **sink** you into the depths of despair that you can only escape by being held hostage by releasing the **shackles** of dysfunction."

Day 173

"You cannot shame **yourself** for becoming the person that others want **you** to be."

Day 174

"You will meet people that come into your **life**, and their eyes will be open, and they do not see you; they **hear** but refuse to **listen**, shun them."

Day 175

"You can't shame **yourself** for becoming a person you do **not want** to be."

Day 176

"There are puzzles in people you **meet** that you will solve that will open doors to **puzzles** in them that you may never **solve**."

Day 177

"If you work around a significant number of **women**, you will be judged **daily**, **consistently**, and **endlessly**. Get accustomed to it: Do not take it personally; let it go, get over yourself, and **move on**."

Day 178

"I believe throughout my **life**, I have always had a realistic view of **myself**: I can always be replaced; that is why I strive to be the best version of **myself**, so that in attempting to replace me, I want it to be as **difficult** as possible."

Day 179

"The emotional **pains** of our past need to be acknowledged and healed; **failure** to **heal** from your past can be transmitted to your **spouse**, **children**, and even **friends**."

Day 180

"I have met far too many **individuals** who value someone else's life, yet do not cherish their **own** life."

Day 181

"The **legal** system does not **reward** good behavior; it punishes any behavior that appears **suspicious**."

Day 182

"What you **see** is what you get? How about you can only know **someone** by what they let you **see**?"

Day 183

"**Men or women** in leadership positions have an extraordinarily frail **ego**, like a house of cards or a glass menagerie; one verbal **misstep** and they **crumble**."

Day 184

"Incorporate **rest** and **reflection** every day into your life. Working at your highest level during your day is not **sustainable**. You need to do this because no one in your life or in **corporate America** will tell you to slow down."

Day 185

"Embrace struggles in **life**. These struggles teach you who **you** are and what **you** can overcome."

Day 186

"Your most **painful betrayals** will not come from your **enemies**; they will come from the people you **trust** the most."

Day 187

"In our youth, what people say to us is **essential**, with **wisdom**. What people don't say in a conversation is far more important."

Day 188

"A **woman** takes a selfie in front of a mirror, always looks cute. A **man** takes a selfie of himself in the mirror; you know, he probably lives with his mother and works at **'Bates' motel—creepy."**

Day 189

"Sometimes, you need to **lose** a few battles before you **win** a war."

Day 190

"Just because you have the **right** ingredients for success in **life**, it doesn't necessarily mean you know how to cook."

Day 191

"Struggles create **strong** men and peaceful times for others, ultimately creating **weak** men."

Day 192

"There are **times** when it can be exhausting to carry another man's **burden**."

Day 193

"The **United States** is ranked number one in the world in the number of persons **physically incarcerated**; the far greater concern is the number of **Americans** who are mentally and emotionally incarcerated."

Day 194

"There will be many people you meet on your journey who will only **love you** if you suppress yourself for them. They can only **love** or **respect** you if they accept you as **inferior** to them. They can only suppress you so they can elevate themselves above you to elevate their **self-esteem**."

Day 195

"You will never meet someone in life who **mistreats** you and is **emotionally** stable."

Day 196

"There will be times in your **life** that you will meet people who can **influence** your **life**; however, when you meet them, it may be the wrong time."

Day 197

"One of life's greatest lessons was when I stopped **expecting** my **principles** and **values** from others."

Day 198

"The priority of getting **older** is to have memories, not **unfulfilled dreams**."

Day 199

"The secret to happiness? Your **children and family** are dumbasses."

Day 200

"You never learn who you are, what you **believe** in, your **values**, inner **strength**, what you will stand for, and what you won't stand for until you have **struggled** in life."

Day 201

"Most of us are so tied to the **past harms** that we cannot let go of our **experiences** to become the person we want to be in the **future**."

Day 202

"Having a **strong work ethic** is always in constant opposition to a **rest ethic**."

Day 203

"Even before I had children, I knew to never push my unfulfilled visions onto their **dreams** and **aspirations**. They need to find their own **visions** on their own terms."

Day 204

"The human **existence** requires us to be repeatedly **exposed** to bad situations so that we **learn** to avoid those very conditions that got us there."

Day 205

"From the **corporate world** and my **personal life**, I have learned that if your **boss** or a **significant** other does not listen to you, they just **don't care** about you."

Day 206

"With wisdom in **human interactions**, I have learned to see things that may not be visible and to hear things that are unsaid."

Day 207

"I have served **humanity** by solving their heart problems. In life, when I often hear complaints, I always ask, **'So what is the solution**?' And then they **shut up**."

Day 208

"Anger is an emotion that can be a **superpower**. When used to motivate oneself, **superhuman** goals can be accomplished. When we hold on to this emotion, it can **destroy** us and those close to us. True growth can only come from harnessing **anger** for good and eventually letting it go and moving on."

Day 209

"We can look back on our past with **disappointment** and **shame**, or choose to embrace it with gratitude. This optic allows us to see our future, with **grace** or **fear**."

Day 210

"**I** have met people who have a myopic view of the world; unfortunately, **they** cannot see the world through any other lens than their **own**."

Day 211

"It took adulthood to embrace my past **struggles** and **pains**; those are a part of who I am, and I am proud to own those struggles."

Day 212

"It takes great wisdom to bring **chaos** and **confusion** and convert them to **order** and **clairvoyance**."

Day 213

"I am not very attracted to women who **love** or **resemble** Honey Boo Boo's mama."

Day 214

"I have finally **learned** to connect words with my **feelings** and now better understand **humanity**."

Day 215

"The most essential superpower as a cardiologist is to be able to compartmentalize your emotions during your patient's sudden death, to think **quickly**, **clearly**, and **decisively**, and to execute your next steps to bring them **back to life**."

Day 216

"Sometimes in life, **expectations** may be the most significant breeding ground for **disappointments**."

Day 217

"In the **corporate** and **academic worlds**, many leaders still fail to understand that giving public praise may be far more important than giving a raise."

Day 218

"There were many times during my **career development** when I felt like I **traveled alone**. I did so frequently that I became **comfortable** being **uncomfortable**. I was never in despair because my **ego** did not drive me; I was driven by the need to do well for my **patient**."

Day 219

"We were all taught to believe that **money** talks; that was a lie, **money** yells!!"

Day 220

"Far too many people in **leadership** positions fail to **appreciate** or **understand** the talent of those who report to them."

Day 221

"Art **propagates** the lessons of our **civilization** while governments keep us in **ignorance**."

Day 222

"The most common phrase I have heard in the **American lexicon** has been **'toxic masculinity'**; we have all **met** or **dealt** with a man with these traits. In a small circle of my friends, we discussed the importance of equality and used the phrase **'toxic femininity**.' This also needs to be clearly defined."

Day 223

"Nothing is more **dangerous** than a man who **has nothing to lose**."

- Inspired by James Baldwin

Day 224

"Honesty of our friendship; I would rather you **hate** me for telling you the truth and become better than you **love** me for telling you a **lie**, and you stay the same and never change."

Day 225

"Based on what I have seen and heard, **life** can be **beautiful** and **cruel**. Both statements are correct based on my experiences in life. We choose how to see, **listen**, and **respond** daily to the world around us."

Day 226

"We are always and **forever** in our children's eyes. Remember to **live** for someone greater than **yourself**."

Day 227

"We place far too much weight on the altar of expert opinions, **social media**, and **celebrity** or **famous** sound bites. We need to go back to our basic beliefs of right and wrong we learned in our first decade of **life**."

Day 228

"**We** all want what we don't have; few **appreciate** what we do have."

Day 229

"Tragedies are part of our **human condition**, bringing **opportunities** for **learning** and **wisdom**, or for **denial** and **ignorance**."

Day 230

"I have developed a new definition for relationship: a state in which two individuals **peacefully** and **respectfully** interact through mutual compromise."

Day 231

"Societies have a major personality flaw we all carry within us; **Judgement** is always so much easier than **understanding**."

Day 232

"The most **essential words** in any relationship: I **forgive** you, I am **sorry**."

Day 233

"There have been many times in life's situations that I may not **say** much, but I see **everything**. I have learned to become **quite comfortable** with the idea that there is **'wisdom in silence'**."

Day 234

"**Sometimes** things will work out in **life**, even when they may not seem **fair**."

Day 235

"There will be times in your **life** where your **emotional pain** will be your **strength**, **leverage** your past to create your **future**."

Day 236

"I have grown **accepting** and **comfortable** hearing things I don't want to hear."

Day 237

"I no longer define the struggles of **life** as my **difficulties**; I describe them as my **resilience**."

Day 238

"Not every **comment** on social media needs my **response**. Will my comments in any way **help** the situation?"

Day 239

"The world is a far **safer place** because never in my **life** have I worn a pair of '**skinny jeans**.'"

Day 240

"Apparently, I will interact daily with others who are always seeking an **emotionally safe place**. Does that even exist? Those who report to me and those I report to are rarely interested in an **emotionally safe space**."

Day 241

"There will be individuals in your **work** and **personal** life who will not like you for many **superficial reasons** and will make your life extraordinarily difficult; do they deserve your **time** and **energy**? Is it my **problem** or theirs? Who **cares** anyway?"

Day 242

"**Humanity** has made extraordinary technological growth but little **emotional development**; we still fight wars and cannot **resolve daily conflicts** with civility."

Day 243

"**People** are so much more than the **bad** things that happen to them."

Day 244

"A large population of Americans has difficulty managing **expectations** and **reality**. My experiences in medicine have taught me that **expectations** never meet reality, even for the ultra-successful. So I have become quite comfortable with the fact that many of the efforts I put into my craft will seldom be praised, so I love with gratitude for every obstacle I conquer in quiet **humility**."

Day 245

"I have reached unprecedented levels of **national** and **international success**; when I retrace my steps, I cannot verbalize how I got here; I resort to words of vigorous **hard work**. I could always outwork anyone and had the heart of an explorer."

Day 246

"The American culture has little **patience** and **expectations**; we want it now, and who cares about the **future**? I have an innate gift for patience and a **long-term vision**."

Day 247

"The **truth** can be so **painful** to hear. It is much **easier** to accept our **reality** with denial."

Day 248

"What I do for a **living** is extraordinarily abstract to many people. I am constantly managing an imminent **threat** of death in a **patient** or managing a patient's **death** and keeping them **alive**; unless you are in the room, you don't understand, and I am all right with that."

Day 249

"If you are **afraid** of offending others, you will never be able to tell the **truth**."

Day 250

"Creating **wealth** has never been about how much you **earn**; it's about how much you save and not **spend** and **invest** over time."

Day 251

"Leaving a toxic relationship shows **resilience** and **courage**, not a sign of **weakness** or **meekness**."

Day 252

"It takes a **lifetime** to **accept** who you are finally."

Day 253

"The best way to **understand** others is to **listen** to them."

Day 254

"**Competence** and **confidence** are interrelated. I have seen far too much **confidence** without competence."

Day 255

"We cannot fix past **injustices** with current **injustices**."

Day 256

"I am **responsible** for what I say, not what you **understand**."

Day 257

"Having a baby to **'save marriage'** is not a strategy; **it's stupidity**."

Day 258

"There are people I have met that you can ask the **time** and they tell you how to **build a fucking watch**."

Day 259

"Why does it seem like the most **unattractive** girls are the most **worried** they are getting hit on?"

Day 260

"I have many **superpowers**, but I also have some **weaknesses**. My kryptonite is a woman with a British accent. I hear one, and I start taking off my clothes."

Day 261

"You can deny yourself so many **experiences** and **opportunities** in life simply because you are **afraid** to ask for help."

Day 262

"I have always **worked** with a chip on my shoulder, and I am alright with this."

Day 263

"You will meet people who decide your **value**, **intelligence**, **capabilities**, and **potential** based solely on what their eyes allow them to see."

Day 264

"**Success** in your profession is being so good at your **craft** that they cannot ignore you."

Day 265

"The most profound moments of **hardship** and **suffering** can be significant for **self-growth and knowledge**."

Day 266

"**Resentment** is a **heavy** load to carry through life; the **burden** becomes light with **forgiveness**."

Day 267

"Sometimes in life, you will **win** by **losing**."

Day 268

"The body of work that you have done over your **lifetime** determines what you will accomplish."

Day 269

"One of my greatest lessons from a very young time in my **life** continues to be validated: we rarely directly **benefit** from our **good deeds** for others and our children. In the work environment, we seldom see these **benefits**. The lack of direct benefits neither drives nor deters my desire to improve the lives of those I care about."

Day 270

"I have developed an inner **intensity** switch. When it is 1 o'clock in the morning, and I am called for an emergency, I can **awaken** and become combat-ready to perform **life-saving procedures**."

Day 271

"Good humans **build** and **lift** others; flawed humans **destroy** and **oppress** others."

Day 272

"If you seek **authenticity**, pay less attention to what people think of you."

Day 273

"You cannot **decide** who I am based on your eyesight."

Day 274

"There will be some **obstacles** in your life; the best way around them may be to go through them."

Day 275

"We can **invest** so much time trying to make our lives perfect and be **disappointed** by imperfections. I find great **fulfillment** when life events are less than ideal. **Good** is still better than **perfect**."

Day 276

"One of life's greatest inconsistencies is to fulfill your time on earth. You cannot **run** from life's **problems**; we must **confront** life's **problems** head-on and with extraordinary ferocity."

Day 277

"Once you reach a certain level of **success**, you **realize** how little you need to be **happy**."

Day 278

"**Discipline**, in many situations, can trump intelligence. I have met many intelligent people who stifled their **potential** because of **laziness** and a **lack of discipline**."

Day 279

"The only way to extract your **self-doubt** is to work it out of yourself."

Day 280

"People can only see you as you are at this **moment** and **time**; few can ever truly understand the challenges, **peaks**, and **valleys** you descended and climbed to accomplish your **goals**."

Day 281

"**Self-control** and **self-awareness** are your greatest **strengths** in determining your **destiny**."

Day 282

"My best **strength** in life was when I reached a point in my life when my mood was unfazed based on the insignificant **toxicity** and actions of others."

Day 283

"Never allow others to **control** your **destiny**."

Day 284

"Many in your life will test your **ability** to control your **emotions** over your **intelligence**."

Day 285

"There is a difference between someone breaking your **heart** and breaking your **expectations**. It's up to you to figure out which one."

Day 286

"Your **material possessions** should never own your soul."

Day 287

"The other day, while out and about, I overheard a young man say, 'If all they ever see in me is bad, what is the **motivation** for me to ever be good? This reminded me of the development of our morale. Our family, friends, and religion shape our values. When that fails, what is the responsibility of schools and the community in shaping our values?"

Day 288

"I must always close the current chapter in my **life** before I open a new one."

Day 289

"Everyone you meet in life is **fighting a battle** you know nothing about."

Day 290

"The **truth** does not set you free; the **ugly truth** does."

Day 291

"**Eagles don't fly** with chickens. **Eagles don't flock**; you have to find them one at a time."

Day 292

"Sometimes, if you go back far enough in your **past**, you can see your **future**."

Day 293

"I have no **limitations**; society sets those **limitations**, and it is up to you to accept or refute those **limitations**."

Day 294

"Amateurs practice until they get it right, **professionals practice** until they can't get it wrong."

Day 295

"The last thing we saw can tremendously bias us in the **future**."

Day 296

"If there is anything I would like to give my children, it is the **ability to see** them through my eyes."

Day 297

"Heart procedures have a margin of **error** that is very, very small."

Day 298

"In your home, you want to be **loved**; in your work, you want to be **believed**."

Day 299

"My **retirement** comes when my best **effort** is no longer good enough."

Day 300

"Sometimes when I look at **someone** or **something**, I don't always see it as it is, but for what it can be."

Day 301

"Have you ever gone to a **wedding** and you're like, 'So that's your best'?"

Day 302

"The **journey** should be **cherished** and the **destination ignored**."

Day 303

"When a man loses his **dreams**, he ceases to live and merely exists."

Day 304

"Just because you **can**, it doesn't mean you **should**."

Day 305

"Don't ever let **another person** tell your **history**."

Day 306

"Even a **broken watch** is right twice per day."

Day 307

"**Failure** does not make you a **loser**; it makes you human."

Day 308

"There is no shortage of people who want to take credit for your **great work**, and a far greater number of people who want to **discredit** your **work**."

Day 309

"**Arrogance** and **self-awareness** rarely go together."

Day 310

"There have been times in my career when I had to take **action** and 'let me show these **fuckers** what they are missing'."

Day 311

"The work of a **heart specialist** doesn't change you, it makes you more of who you are."

Day 312

"With a college education, I learned how to learn and **realized** I knew little, with life **experiences**, I learned how to apply what I learned and gained **wisdom**."

Day 313

"I have traveled over **1.5 million miles**; the world has become **small** to me."

Day 314

"I can function and work well because I apparently have a very high **tolerance for ambiguity**."

Day 315

"We all have our battles, one with the person sitting across from you, the second is the **person inside** of you. Once you conquer the one inside of you, the one across from you really doesn't matter."

Day 316

"I have had many times in my life and career when I had to **work harder** than an **ugly stripper**."

Day 317

"**Working** and **operating** on the heart has a very, very small **margin of error**."

Day 318

"I have never heard someone wake up one morning and say, **working on the heart looks like fun**, I think I will make a living working in conditions where a patient is at continuous risk of imminent death"

Day 319

"**Denial** and **fear** are humans' greatest inner **demons**."

Day 320

"In life, we **perseverate on the negative things**, despite wanting to relive the positive things."

Day 321

"There are times when people speak to me, and I cannot tell if it's a **compliment** or an **insult**."

Day 322

"Some mornings, I wake up and think I might have a striking resemblance to Tommy Lee Jones. I would have said Morgan Freeman, but I am not **attracted** to my granddaughter."

Day 323

"Sometimes your life needs to be **unplugged** and **plugged** back in, what IT calls 'reboot.'"

Day 324

"I have come to embrace the ideology that I may have a **vision** that no one sees but me, I am ok with that."

Day 325

"Throughout my **life**, I have always felt that I was pushing the outer boundaries of my **physical/emotional capacity**."

Day 326

"Do you feel **pushed** in life? I have never felt this; I always thought I was being **pulled** by a force I cannot resist."

Day 327

"My experience with people is that **some individuals** learned that you can be mentally beaten at **any time** for **anything**, and also learned that there is no point in making any **effort** to **avoid** the beatings."

Day 328

"It's not about what **people call you,** it's about what you answer to."

Day 329

"I don't **fear failure**; I am terrified of regret."

Day 330

"Adversity doesn't **build character**, it reveals it."

Day 331

"**Do what you** have **to do**, so that you can do what you want to do."

Day 332

"Sometimes I find **myself** making **SWAG** (scientific wild ass guess)."

Day 333

"Every man can have a **child**, but not every man can be a **father**."

Day 334

"Nothing is heavier than the **grudges**, **dysfunctions**, and **emotional pains** you carry and refuse to let go."

Day 335

"Broken men can also be **extraordinarily dangerous**."

Day 336

"In corporations, it is essential to maintain their values, not to become **institutionalized** and then **radicalized**, not to lose one's objectivity, and to have **blind allegiance**."

Day 337

"Some individuals have had so many **struggles** in life that they do not have dreams; they **plan** and **execute**."

Day 338

"That which makes you **smile** can also make you **cry**."

Day 339

"There is a gray line in your **life experience** between the end of something and the beginning of another."

Day 340

"You are not what **happens** to you unless you **allow** it."

Day 341

"**One sincere person** in your life is more valuable than **1000 superficial acquaintances**."

Day 342

"It can be challenging to **trust** what others say, so learn to **trust** your ability to **recognize** others' patterns of **dysfunctional behavior**."

Day 343

"Make no room in your **heart** or **life** for the people who have **broken you**."

Day 344

"Be accountable to yourself, make **excuses**, and **destroy** your character."

Day 345

"There were several **times in my life** when I had to leave experiences behind and thought I would die, when in fact I was reborn."

Day 346

"The more ignorant you are **throughout life**, the **happier** you will be; the more you **understand** about life, the more **difficult your existence**."

Day 347

"Once you wake up and **understand life**, you can never go back to **sleep again**."

Day 348

"It is much easier to hear about someone else's **lies** than to listen to our own **truths**."

Day 349

"Allowing words to **control** you empowers others to control you."

Day 350

"To find your inner peace, **see** and **conquer** your inner demons."

Day 351

"You have mastered your **life** when your inner voice is **louder** than the negative **external voices**."

Day 352

"You will always have more enemies when you **succeed** than when you **fail**."

Day 353

"Many times in your life, the best **decisions** are the ones you don't make."

Day 354

"We ll have **hard times**. Some people have it more complicated than others or you."

Day 355

"If you want to be successful, **befriend** and **spend time** with people who are what you want to be."

Day 356

"A large part of my **success** was built on the backs and shoulders of those who could not outwork me."

Day 357

"I have had an infinite amount of **success in life**, not because of **high intelligence**; I was gifted with an **abundance of common sense**."

Day 358

"**Success** can only be **achieved** by running towards what you want and away from what you fear."

Day 359

"It can be so easy to recognize and dislike flaws in others, yet so **complex** and **challenging** to identify weaknesses within us."

Day 360

"**Freedom** is on the other side of **financial success**."

Day 361

"The **worst day** of your life is when the person you are meets the person you could have been."

Day 362

"Peace comes when you have **faced and conquered** your inner demons."

Day 363

"Those around you will not **universally celebrate** your **success**."

Day 364

"The law of conservation of energy states that energy can neither be **created nor destroyed** but is **transferred** from one form to **another**: from the US economy. Money can be **made** and **destroyed**; money moves from one person to another. There is a finite amount of money in the United States unless added from other countries' economies."

Day 365

"**Society** and **American culture** have failed themselves; we have been unable to recognize how little encouragement an **individual** needs to cope with **stress** from **work** or **home life**, from their spouses or significant others."

About the Author

I am Jean-Bernard Durand, MD, FACC, FACP, FCCP, FAHA, FHFSA, FHRS, FHFA, FRCP, a tenured professor at The University of Texas MD Anderson Cancer Center, an adjunct professor at Texas A&M University, and a voluntary staff cardiologist at Baylor College of Medicine.

I have held clinical appointments at Texas Heart Institute/Baylor St. Luke's, the University of Texas Hermann Memorial Hospital, and The Methodist Hospital.

I am a certified executive and life coach. I immigrated to the United States from the Caribbean and have lived in New York City, San Diego, Wisconsin, Palo Alto, Chicago, and Houston, Texas.

I completed training in both the clinical and basic sciences. During my internal medicine residency at Loyola University School of Medicine in Chicago, I pursued advanced research training. I completed an American Heart Association/Bugher Foundation Fellowship in molecular biology, investigating hypertrophic and dilated cardiomyopathy.

Under the mentorship of Dr. Robert Roberts, known as the father of molecular cardiology, I was awarded a Robert Wood Johnson Fellowship in molecular genetics at Baylor College of Medicine. This work led to the localization of a gene on chromosome 1q32 and the identification of troponin as one of the first genes associated with familial dilated cardiomyopathy.

Following my cardiology fellowship at Baylor College of Medicine, I completed additional clinical training in immunology, advanced heart failure, circulatory support, and cardiac transplantation. I served as Assistant Medical Director of the Heart Transplant Service at Baylor.

I was recruited to MD Anderson Cancer Center to establish a cardiomyopathy program and a fully integrated interventional cardiology service. I was the first to develop a cardiomyopathy service within a cancer hospital, setting standards for cardioprotection prior to anthracycline-based therapies and investigating mechanisms of cardiac recovery in chemotherapy- and radiation-induced cardiomyopathy.

I developed the world's largest DNA and tissue bank for chemotherapy-induced cardiomyopathy to identify genetic polymorphisms predicting heart failure risk. I also established the first cardiac device clinic at MD Anderson, using mobile device monitoring for patients with arrhythmias and heart failure.

I have authored more than 100 peer-reviewed publications and have served as an IRB co-chair for over 20 years. I am a national and international speaker in cardio-oncology, a member of the American Heart Association Cardio-Oncology Council, and serve as a co-principal investigator on multiple clinical trials for stem cell therapy in anthracycline-induced cardiomyopathy.

Outside of medicine, I am an avid reader and lifelong student of learning. I hold a second-degree black belt in Tae Kwon Do, have trained in Kung Fu, boxing, and combat sports, completed six marathons, and enjoy photography.

I am the proud father of two children: JP Durand and Samantha Durand.

www.ingramcontent.com/pod-product-compliance
Ingram Content Group UK Ltd.
Pitfield, Milton Keynes, MK11 3LW, UK
UKHW062003290726
14090UKWH00022B/1360

9 781966 968795